SCHOLASTI

D1489527

Fun Flaps
Phonics

Immacula A. Rhodes

NEW YORK • TORONTO • LONDON • AUCKLAND • SYDNEY
MEXICO CITY • NEW DELHI • HONG KONG • BUENOS AIRES

Teaching *Resources*

Text on pages 4–6 adapted from *Fun-Flap Facts: Multiplication* by Danielle Blood.
Copyright © 2004 by Danielle Blood. Used by permission of Scholastic Teaching Resources.

Cover design by Maria Lilja
Interior design by Kathy Massaro

ISBN: 978-0-545-28079-2

5 6 7 8 9 10   40   18 17 16 15 14 13

Contents

Phonics Fun Flaps

Initial Consonants

Short Vowels

Long Vowels

Diphthongs, Variant Vowels, & R-Controlled Vowels

Consonant Blends & Digraphs

Introduction

Welcome to *Fun Flaps: Phonics*, a hands-on way to help children practice essential reading skills. This book includes 32 reproducible fun flaps that feature the same interactive format that children know and love. Fun flaps are ideal for learning centers or for use during transition times—in the morning, before or after lunch, at the end of the day, or for practice at home.

Each fun flap features four related phonics skills. Children choose a picture and name it, then lift the flap to reveal that word and additional words that share the same phonics concept. You'll also find additional reproducible pages to make using the fun flaps even easier:

* step-by-step directions for folding the fun flaps (page 6)
* a checklist to help children keep track of the fun flaps they've done (page 7)
* self-checking quizzes (pages 8–15)
* a fun flap template for children to make their own fun flaps (page 48)

The engaging format and illustrations encourage children to review skills again and again. Mastering phonics has never been so much fun!

How to Use This Book

There are many ways these fun flaps can be used in the classroom and at home. Here are some teaching tips to get started.

* Make copies of the fun flaps, store them in labeled hanging files, and place in a learning center. After demonstrating how to fold the fun flaps, post the folding directions nearby. (Many children know how to fold these, but the directions will guide them if questions arise.)

* Have children decorate individualized pocket folders to use for storing their fun flaps, checklists, and quizzes. Explain how to use the checklist to keep track of which fun flaps children have used and to record their quiz scores.

* Brainstorm with children a list of ways that they might support a productive environment in the classroom while using the fun flaps—for example, speaking in low voices when reading and answering the questions.

Introduce a new fun flap each week. Write the number and the featured phonics concept of the fun flap on a sheet of art paper. Then list words that contain the targeted phonics skills. Draw or glue on pictures to go with the words. Invite children to read each word and point out its corresponding picture.

After working with each fun flap, ask children to cut out the self-checking quiz and fold back the right side to hide the answers. Have them complete the quiz and check their work. Then show children how to record their quiz scores on the checklist.

Using the Fun Flaps

1 Partner A holds the fun flap in a closed position, so that the points touch. Partner A asks Partner B to choose a picture on a flap.

2 Partner B selects one of the four pictures.

3 Partner A opens and closes the fun flap the number of times shown above the selected picture, ending with the fun flap in an open position. Partner A holds the fun flap so Partner B can view the four pictures and the corresponding words (with missing letters).

4 Partner B chooses a picture and names it. Partner A lifts the flap to reveal the complete spelling of the word and reads aloud the other words beneath the flap.

5 Partners can switch roles at any point. Practice continues until both partners have taken several turns and are familiar with the phonics concept featured on the fun flap.

Fun Flap Folding Directions

1 Trim off the top part of the fun flap page.

2 Place the fun flap on a flat surface with the blank side facing up.

3 Fold back the four corners along the solid lines so that they touch in the center of the square.

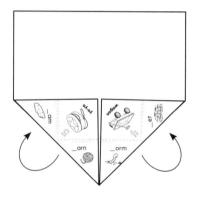

4 Turn over the fun flap. Fold back the corners again so that they touch the center of the square.

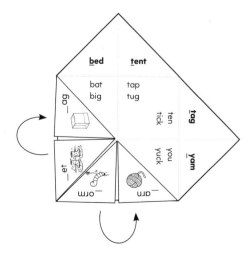

5 Fold the fun flap in half.

6 Place your right thumb and index finger in the right side.

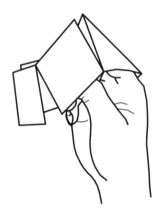

7 Place your left thumb and index finger in the left side.

8 Open and close the fun flap by moving your fingers.

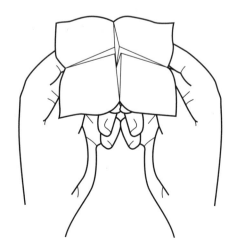

Name _____

Mark an X under "Fun Flap Practice" after you have practiced with the fun flap.
Mark an X under "Quiz" after you have taken the quiz.
Record your quiz score (how many correct out of 8).

	Fun Flap	Fun Flap Practice	Quiz	Score
Initial Consonants	1 **Time for Fun** (b, t, w, y)			
	2 **Perfect Pets** (f, h, l, t)			
	3 **Animal Talk** (b, p, r, w)			
	4 **On the Ground** (g, l, r, s)			
	5 **Field Trip!** (f, m, p, z)			
	6 **Thirst Quenchers** (j, m, s, t)			
	7 **On the Move** (h, j, k, r)			
	8 **Baked Goodies** (b, c, d, m)			
Short Vowels	9 **Creatures, Large and Small** (initial vowels: a, e, i, o)			
	10 **Body Parts on the Move** (a, e, i, u)			
	11 **At the Pond** (a, i, o, u)			
	12 **Around the House** (e, i, o, u)			
	13 **Traveling Along** (a, e, i, u)			
	14 **Dressing Baby** (a, e, i, o)			
Long Vowels	15 **Animal Homes** (silent e)			
	16 **All for Fun** (silent e)			
	17 **Helpful Holders** (silent e)			
	18 **All Wet** (vowel digraphs: ai, ay)			
	19 **Going for a Ride** (vowel digraphs: ea, ee)			
	20 **Wintry Day** (long o)			
Diphthongs, Variant Vowels & R-Controlled Vowels	21 **Working the Farm** (oi, ou, ow, oy)			
	22 **Places to Go** (oo as in moon)			
	23 **In Fashion** (ar, ir, or, ur)			
	24 **City Sights** (ar, ir, or)			
Consonant Blends & Digraphs	25 **The Great Outdoors** (cl, fl, gr, tr)			
	26 **Making Music** (dr, fl, st, tr)			
	27 **Let's Play!** (fl, sk, sl, sw)			
	28 **In the Kingdom** (cr, dr, pr, qu)			
	29 **Cool Critters** (cr, fl, gr, sn)			
	30 **Ready to Eat** (gl, pl, sp, tr)			
	31 **Little Things** (ch, sh, th, wh)			
	32 **All About Tools** (ch, sh, wh)			

1

Name _____ Date _____

Fill in the missing letters. Then write each word.
Use the letters in the box to help you.

b   t   w   y

1. __ent _____

2. __ag _____

3. __arn _____

4. __ed _____

5. __et _____

6. __am _____

7. __op _____

8. __orm _____

1. tent
2. bag
3. yarn
4. bed
5. wet
6. yam
7. top
8. worm

Fold back here.

2

Name _____ Date _____

Fill in the missing letters. Then write each word.
Use the letters in the box to help you.

f   h   l   t

1. __op _____

2. __an _____

3. __eaf _____

4. __ouse _____

5. __ub _____

6. __eg _____

7. __at _____

8. __ive _____

1. top
2. fan
3. leaf
4. house
5. tub
6. leg
7. hat
8. five

Fold back here.

3

Name _____ Date _____

Fill in the missing letters. Then write each word.
Use the letters in the box to help you.

b   p   r   w

1. __eb _____

2. __ine _____

3. __an _____

4. __et _____

5. __op _____

6. __ig _____

7. __ouse _____

8. __ig _____

1. web
2. nine
3. pan
4. net
5. mop
6. pig
7. mouse
8. wig

Fold back here.

4

Name _____ Date _____

Fill in the missing letters. Then write each word.
Use the letters in the box to help you.

g   l   r   s

1. __ain _____

2. __ate _____

3. __aw _____

4. __og _____

5. __un _____

6. __ip _____

7. __um _____

8. __amp _____

1. rain
2. gate
3. saw
4. log
5. sun
6. rip
7. gum
8. lamp

Fold back here.

5 Name _____ Date _____

Fill in the missing letters. Then write each word.
Use the letters in the box to help you.

f	m	p	z

1. ___oot _____   1. foot
2. ___ie _____   2. pie
3. ___ebra _____   3. zebra
4. ___an _____   4. fan
5. ___at _____   5. mat
6. ___ipper _____   6. zipper
7. ___oon _____   7. moon
8. ___ear _____   8. pear

Fold back here.

6 Name _____ Date _____

Fill in the missing letters. Then write each word.
Use the letters in the box to help you.

j	m	s	t

1. ___an _____   1. man
2. ___ar _____   2. jar
3. ___able _____   3. table
4. ___eep _____   4. jeep
5. ___ub _____   5. tub
6. ___eal _____   6. seal
7. ___oap _____   7. soap
8. ___eat _____   8. meat

Fold back here.

7 Name _____ Date _____

Fill in the missing letters. Then write each word.
Use the letters in the box to help you.

h	j	k	r

1. ___orn _____   1. horn
2. ___am _____   2. jam
3. ___ain _____   3. rain
4. ___ing _____   4. king
5. ___ock _____   5. rock
6. ___at _____   6. hat
7. ___ite _____   7. kite
8. ___ug _____   8. jug

Fold back here.

8 Name _____ Date _____

Fill in the missing letters. Then write each word.
Use the letters in the box to help you.

b	c	d	m

1. ___og _____   1. dog
2. ___ee _____   2. bee
3. ___outh _____   3. mouth
4. ___ox _____   4. box
5. ___ot _____   5. cot
6. ___esk _____   6. desk
7. ___an _____   7. can
8. ___ap _____   8. map

Fold back here.

9

Name _____ Date _____

Fill in the missing vowels. Then write each word.
Use the letters in the box to help you.

a   e   i   o

1. __pple _____   1. apple
2. __lf _____   2. elf
3. __nt _____   3. ant
4. __nch _____   4. inch
5. __live _____   5. olive
6. __gloo _____   6. igloo
7. __gg _____   7. egg
8. __n _____   8. on

Fold back here.

10

Name _____ Date _____

Fill in the missing vowels. Then write each word.
Use the letters in the box to help you.

a   e   i   u

1. r__g _____   1. rug
2. d__sk _____   2. desk
3. pl__m _____   3. plum
4. j__m _____   4. jam
5. n__t _____   5. net
6. p__g _____   6. pig
7. cr__b _____   7. crab
8. l__p _____   8. lip

Fold back here.

11

Name _____ Date _____

Fill in the missing vowels. Then write each word.
Use the letters in the box to help you.

a   i   o   u

1. d__ck _____   1. duck
2. cr__b _____   2. crib
3. f__n _____   3. fan
4. b__x _____   4. box
5. cl__m _____   5. clam
6. fr__g _____   6. frog
7. m__g _____   7. mug
8. m__lk _____   8. milk

Fold back here.

12

Name _____ Date _____

Fill in the missing vowels. Then write each word.
Use the letters in the box to help you.

e   i   o   u

1. s__n _____   1. sun
2. b__d _____   2. bed
3. s__ck _____   3. sock
4. w__g _____   4. wig
5. h__n _____   5. hen
6. l__g _____   6. log
7. p__n _____   7. pin
8. g__m _____   8. gum

Fold back here.

Fun Flaps: Phonics © 2011 by Immacula A. Rhodes, Scholastic Teaching Resources • PAGE 10

13 Name _____ Date _____

Fill in the missing vowels. Then write each word.
Use the letters in the box to help you.

a   e   i   u

1. b__g _____   1. bug
2. j__t _____   2. jet
3. v__n _____   3. van
4. br__ck _____   4. brick
5. w__b _____   5. web
6. t__b _____   6. tub
7. c__b _____   7. cab
8. sh__p _____   8. ship

Fold back here.

14 Name _____ Date _____

Fill in the missing vowels. Then write each word.
Use the letters in the box to help you.

a   e   i   o

1. fl__g _____   1. flag
2. sl__d _____   2. sled
3. p__n _____   3. pan
4. k__d _____   4. kid
5. c__t _____   5. cot
6. s__nk _____   6. sink
7. t__p _____   7. top
8. t__nt _____   8. tent

Fold back here.

15 Name _____ Date _____

Fill in the missing vowels and silent e. Then write the word.

1. d__m__ _____   1. dime
2. c__b__ _____   2. cube
3. sk__t__ _____ 3. skate
4. b__n__ _____   4. bone
5. n__n__ _____   5. nine
6. t__p__ _____   6. tape
7. r__s__ _____   7. rose
8. m__l__ _____   8. mule

Fold back here.

16 Name _____ Date _____

Fill in the missing vowels and silent e. Then write the word.

1. c__n__ _____   1. cone
2. k__t__ _____   2. kite
3. c__k__ _____   3. cake
4. m__c__ _____   4. mice
5. h__s__ _____   5. hose
6. d__v__ _____   6. dive
7. b__k__ _____   7. bike
8. g__t__ _____   8. gate

Fold back here.

17

Name _____ Date _____

Fill in the missing vowels and silent e. Then write the word.

1. wh__l__ _____   1. whale

2. m__l__ _____   2. mule

3. sm__l__ _____   3. smile

4. r__b__ _____   4. robe

5. st__v__ _____   5. stove

6. d__n__ _____   6. dune

7. v__n__ _____   7. vine

8. pl__t__ _____   8. plate

Fold back here.

18

Name _____ Date _____

Fill in the missing vowel pairs. Then write each word.
Use the letters in the box to help you.

ai   ay

1. sn__ __l _____   1. snail

2. r__ __n _____   2. rain

3. j__ __ _____   3. jay

4. tr__ __n _____   4. train

5. tr__ __ _____   5. tray

6. n__ __l _____   6. nail

7. spr__ __ _____   7. spray

8. h__ __ _____   8. hay

Fold back here.

19

Name _____ Date _____

Fill in the missing vowel pairs. Then write each word.
Use the letters in the box to help you.

ea   ee

1. sh__ __p _____   1. sheep

2. tr__ __ _____   2. tree

3. s__ __d _____   3. seed

4. s__ __t _____   4. seat

5. b__ __ _____   5. bee

6. l__ __f _____   6. leaf

7. qu__ __n _____   7. queen

8. kn__ __ _____   8. knee

Fold back here.

20

Name _____ Date _____

Fill in the missing vowel sounds. Then write each word.
Use the letters in the box to help you.

o   oa   ow

1. c__ld _____   1. cold

2. c__ __t _____   2. coat

3. sn__ __ _____   3. snow

4. t__ __ _____   4. tow

5. r__ __d _____   5. road

6. sh__ __ _____   6. show

7. cr__ __ _____   7. crow

8. g__ld _____   8. gold

Fold back here.

Fun Flaps: Phonics © 2011 by Immacula A. Rhodes, Scholastic Teaching Resources ■ PAGE 12

21 Name _____ Date _____

Fill in the missing vowel pairs. Then write each word.
Use the letters in the box to help you.

| oi | ou | ow | oy |

1. c___ ___ _____   1. cow

2. s___ ___l _____   2. soil

3. b___ ___ _____   3. boy

4. pl___ ___ _____   4. plow

5. cl___ ___d _____   5. cloud

6. t___ ___ _____   6. toy

7. h___ ___se _____   7. house

8. c___ ___n _____   8. coin

Fold back here.

---

22 Name _____ Date _____

Fill in the missing vowel pairs. Then write each word.

1. p___ ___l _____   1. pool

2. bl___ ___m _____   2. bloom

3. r___ ___f _____   3. roof

4. b___ ___t _____   4. boot

5. sp___ ___n _____   5. spoon

6. t___ ___th _____   6. tooth

7. st___ ___l _____   7. stool

8. br___ ___m _____   8. broom

Fold back here.

---

23 Name _____ Date _____

Fill in the missing letter pairs. Then write each word.
Use the letters in the box to help you.

| ar | ir | or | ur |

1. g___ ___l _____   1. girl

2. b___ ___n _____   2. burn

3. f___k _____   3. fork

4. p___ ___se _____   4. purse

5. b___ ___d _____   5. bird

6. st___ ___ _____   6. star

7. h___n _____   7. horn

8. b___ ___n _____   8. barn

Fold back here.

---

24 Name _____ Date _____

Fill in the missing letter pairs. Then write each word.
Use the letters in the box to help you.

| ar | ir | or |

1. d___ ___t _____   1. dart

2. c___ ___n _____   2. corn

3. sh___ ___t _____   3. shirt

4. c___ ___ _____   4. car

5. h___ ___se _____   5. horse

6. sh___ ___k _____   6. shark

7. th___ ___d _____   7. third

8. y___ ___n _____   8. yarn

Fold back here.

25

Name _____ Date _____

Fill in the missing letter pairs. Then write each word.
Use the letters in the box to help you.

| cl   fl   gr   tr |

1. __ __ay _____   1. tray
2. __ __ill _____   2. grill
3. __ __ock _____   3. clock
4. __ __ag _____   4. flag
5. __ __ape _____   5. grape
6. __ __am _____   6. clam
7. __ __unk _____   7. trunk
8. __ __oat _____   8. float

Fold back here.

26

Name _____ Date _____

Fill in the missing letter pairs. Then write each word.
Use the letters in the box to help you.

| dr   fl   st   tr |

1. __ __ar _____   1. star
2. __ __ay _____   2. tray
3. __ __ute _____   3. flute
4. __ __um _____   4. drum
5. __ __op _____   5. stop
6. __ __oat _____   6. float
7. __ __ess _____   7. dress
8. __ __uck _____   8. truck

Fold back here.

27

Name _____ Date _____

Fill in the missing letter pairs. Then write each word.
Use the letters in the box to help you.

| fl   sk   sl   sw |

1. __ __ed _____   1. sled
2. __ __ame _____   2. flame
3. __ __ate _____   3. skate
4. __ __ing _____   4. swing
5. __ __ower _____   5. flower
6. __ __unk _____   6. skunk
7. __ __eep _____   7. sleep
8. __ __im _____   8. swim

Fold back here.

28

Name _____ Date _____

Fill in the missing letter pairs. Then write each word.
Use the letters in the box to help you.

| cr   dr   pr   qu |

1. __ __own _____   1. crown
2. __ __um _____   2. drum
3. __ __ize _____   3. prize
4. __ __een _____   4. queen
5. __ __ust _____   5. crust
6. __ __ilt _____   6. quilt
7. __ __ince _____   7. prince
8. __ __ip _____   8. drip

Fold back here.

2 Perfect Pets

Name the picture. Add the beginning sound.
Pick your favorite pet to start.

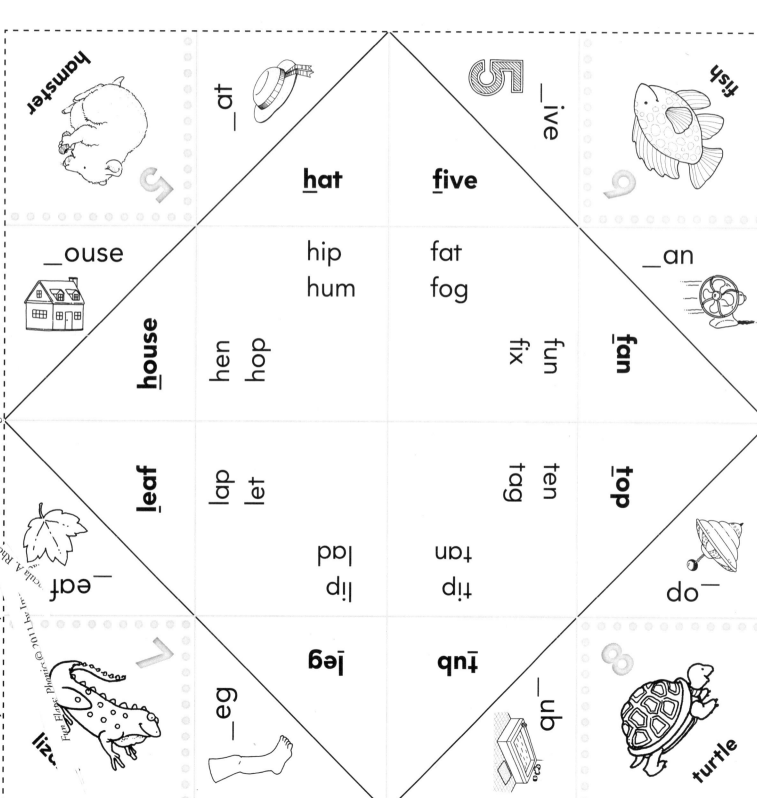

hamster

_at

_ive

fish

_ouse

hat   five

hip   fat

hum   fog

house   hen   hop   fix   fun   _an

leaf   lap   let   tag   ten   **fan**

_eaf   lad   tan   **top**

                  lip   tip

lizard   leg   tub   do_

_eg   _ub   turtle

3 Animal Talk

Name the picture. Add the beginning sound.
Pick your favorite animal sound to start.

baa

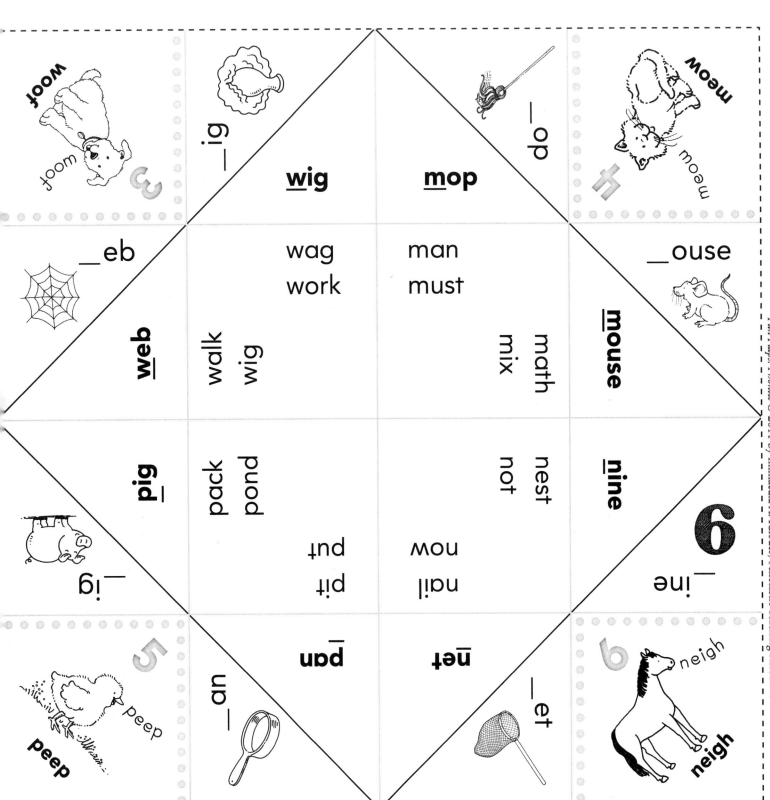

woof

woof

3

_ig

wig

_op

mop

4

meow

meow

_eb

wag

work

man

must

_ouse

web

walk

wig

math

mix

mouse

pig

pack

pond

nest

not

nine

_ig

put

pit

now

nail

9

_ine

5

peep

peep

_an

pan

net

_et

6

neigh

neigh

4 On the Ground

Name the picture. Add the beginning sound.
Pick your favorite thing found on the ground to start.

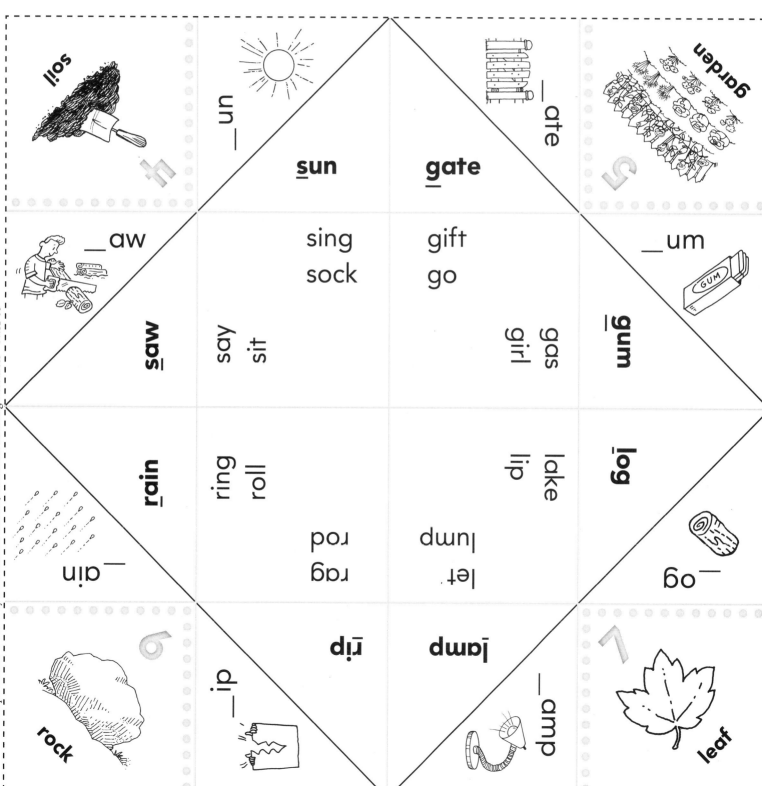

soil
4 _un
_ate
garden 5

_aw
sun   gate
_um

saw
sing   gift
gum

say   sock   go
sit   gas   girl

rain
ring   lake   log
roll   lip

_ain
rod   lump
og

rag   let
rip   lamp

rock 6
_ip
rip   lamp
_amp
leaf 7

5 Field Trip!

Name the picture. Add the beginning sound.
Pick your favorite place to go on a field trip to start.

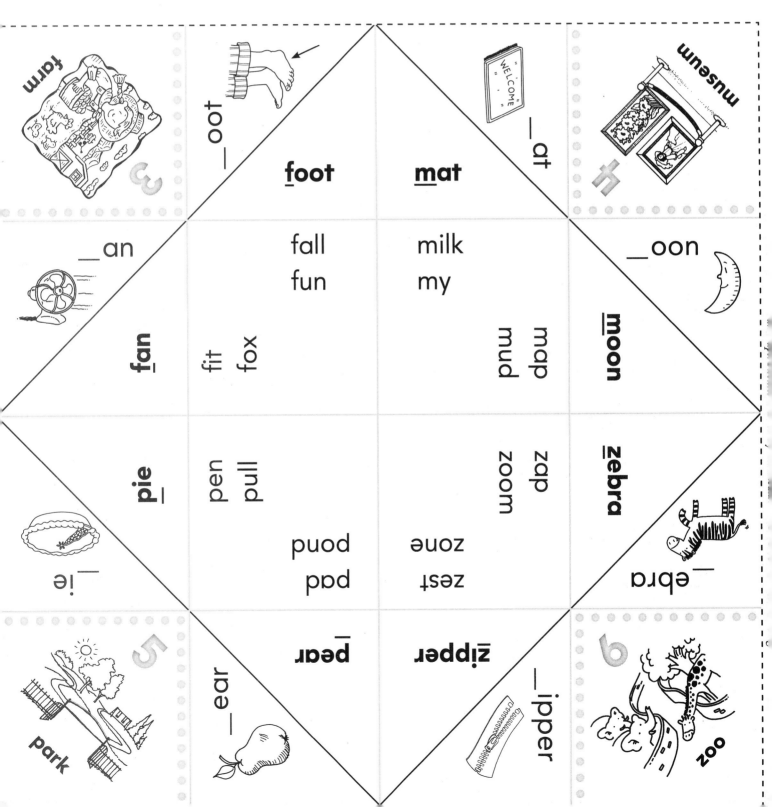

6 Thirst Quenchers

Name the picture. Add the beginning sound.
Pick your favorite drink to start.

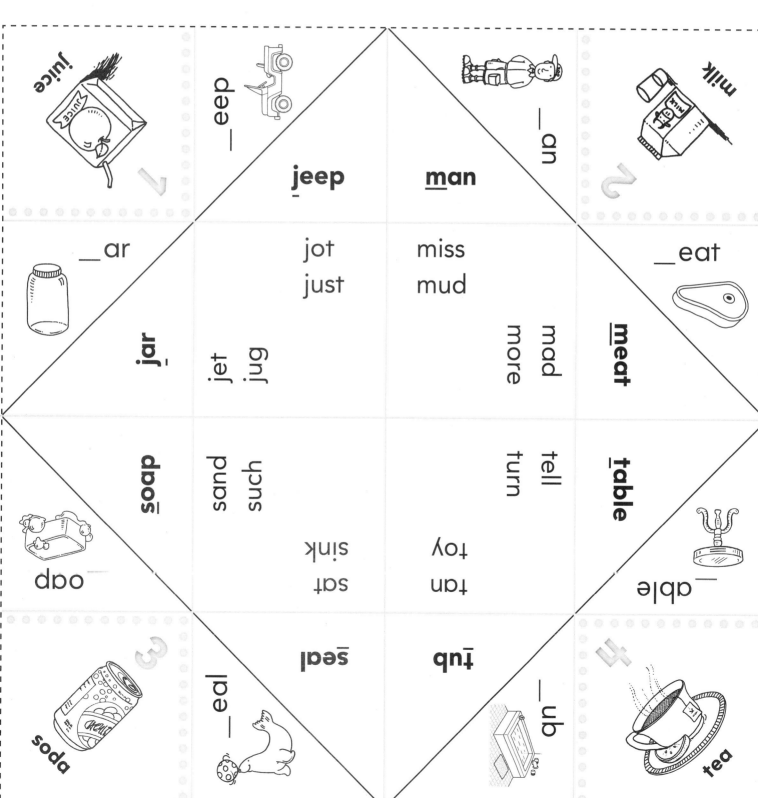

juice

1

_eep

jeep

man

_an

milk

2

_ar

jot
just

miss
mud

_eat

jar

jet
jug

mad
more

meat

soap

sand
such

tell
turn

table

oap

sink
sat

toy
tan

_able

soda

3

_eal

seal

tub

_ub

tea

4

7 On the Move

Name the picture. Add the beginning sound.
Pick your favorite way to move to start.

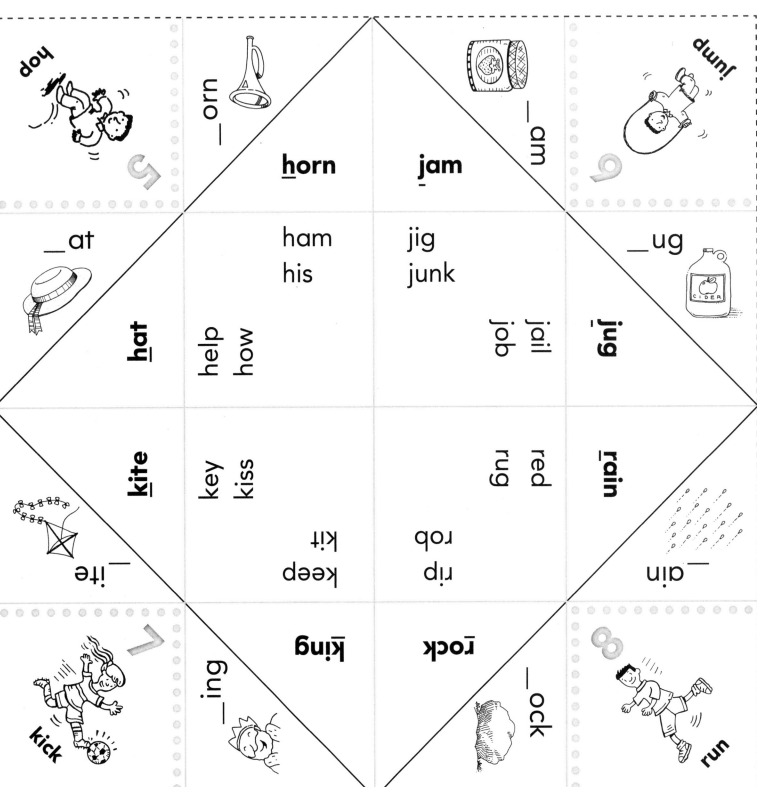

_orn

horn

jam

_am

ham
his

jig
junk

_at

_ug

hat

help
how

jail
job

jug

kite

key
kiss

red
rug

rain

kit
keep

rob
rip

_ain

_ite

king

rock

_ing

_ock

kick

run

8 Baked Goodies

Name the picture. Add the beginning sound.
Pick your favorite baked treat to start.

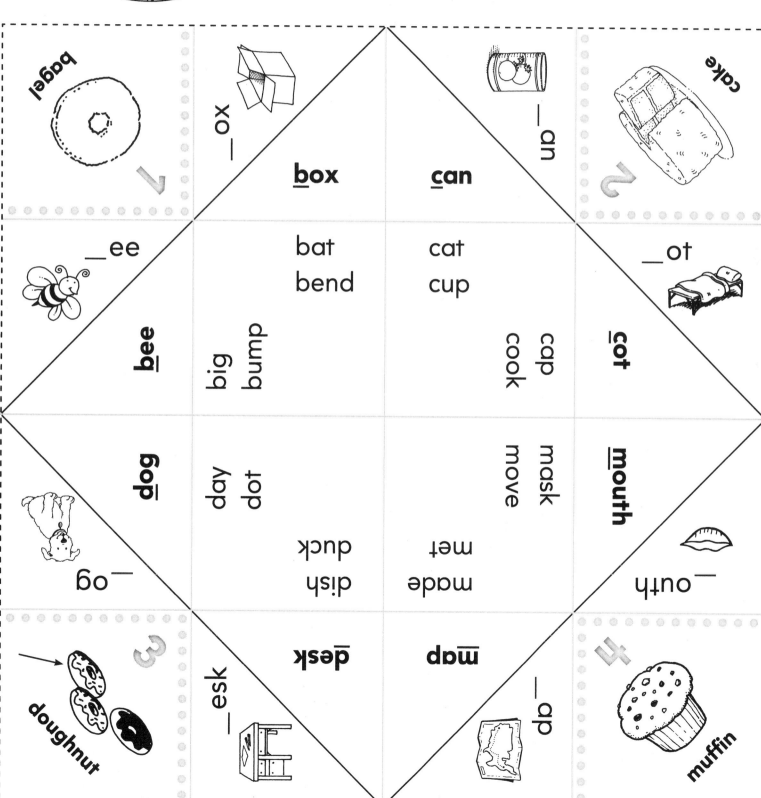

bagel 1

_ox

_ee

bee

dog

_og

doughnut 3

_esk **desk**

box
bat
bend
big bump
day dot
duck dish

_an

can
cat
cup
cap cook
mask move
met made
map

_ap

cake 2

_ot

cot

mouth

_outh

muffin 4

Creatures, Large and Small

Name the picture. Add the beginning vowel sound.
Pick your favorite creature to start.

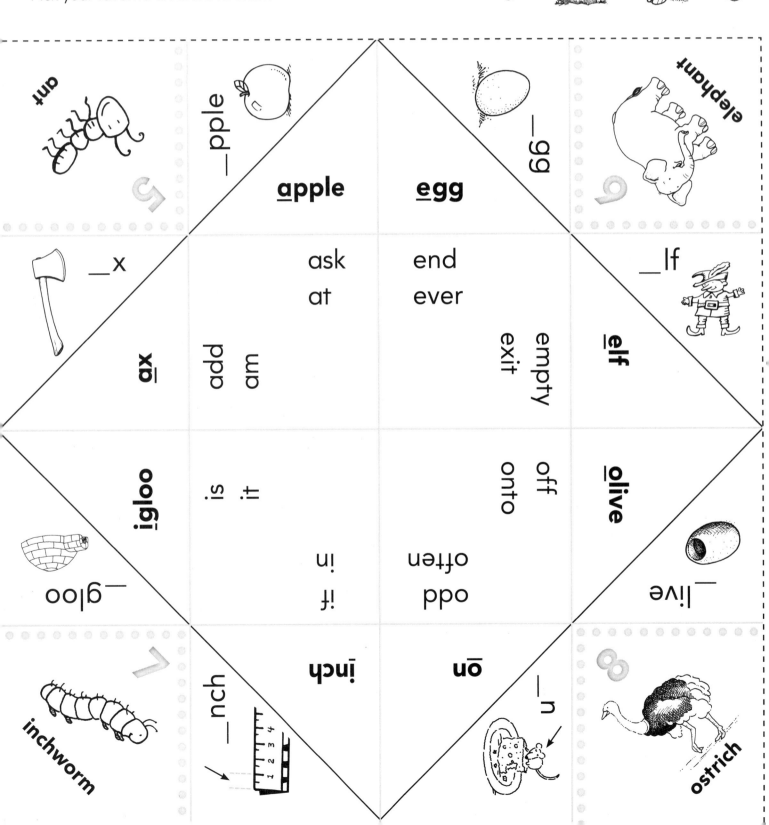

ant

_pple

_gg

elephant

_x

ask
at

end
ever

_lf

ax

add
am

empty
exit

elf

igloo

is
it

off
onto

olive

_gloo

in
if

often
ppo
odd

_live

inchworm

_nch

inch

on

_n

ostrich

apple

egg

10 Body Parts on the Move

Name the picture. Add the vowel sound.
Pick your favorite moveable body part to start.

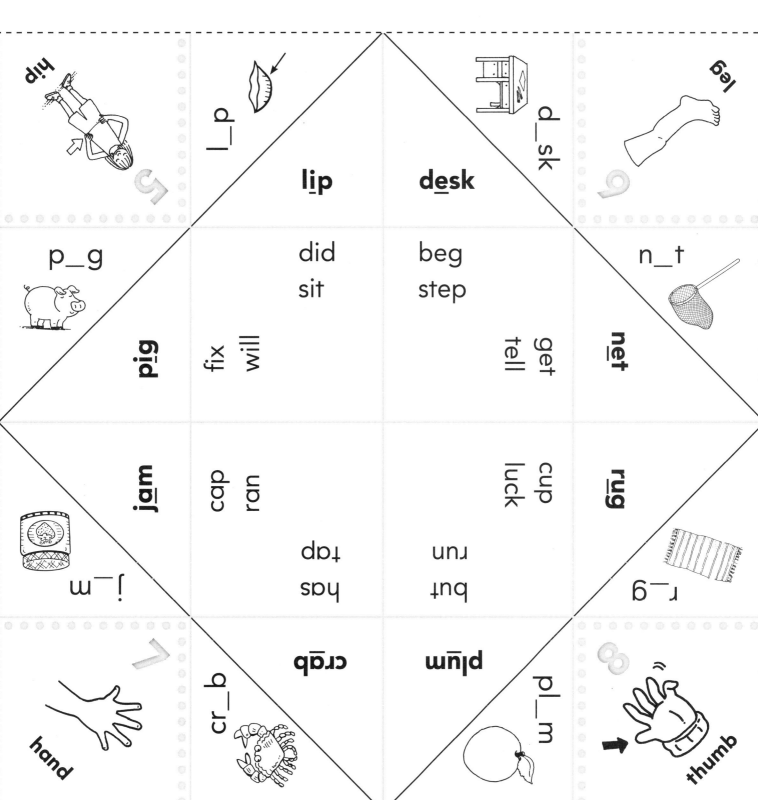

hip

l_p

lip   desk

did   beg

sit   step

d_sk

leg

p_g

pig

fix will

get tell

n_t

net

jam

cap ran

cup luck

rug

j_m

tap   run

has   but

r_g

hand

cr_b

crab   plum

pl_m

thumb

11 At the Pond

Name the picture. Add the vowel sound.
Pick your favorite pond animal to start.

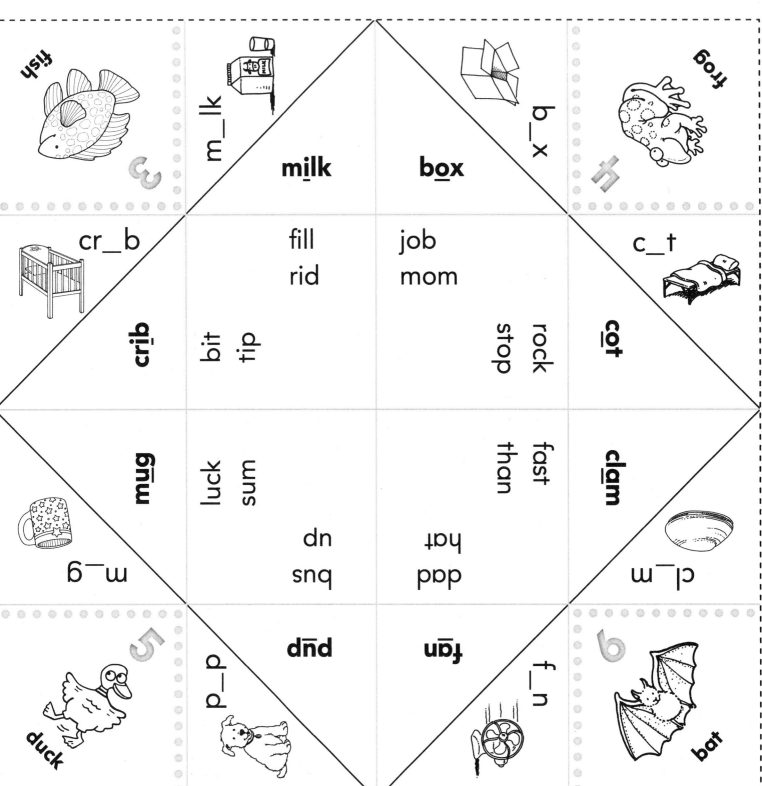

fish 3

m_lk

milk

box

b_x

frog 4

cr_b

fill
rid

job
mom

c_t

crib

bit tip

rock
stop

cot

mug

luck sum

fast
than

clam

m_g

dn
sn q

t ph
p pp

cl_m

duck 5

p_p

dn d

f n t

f_n

bat 6

12 Around the House

Name the picture. Add the vowel sound.
Pick your favorite item around the house to start.

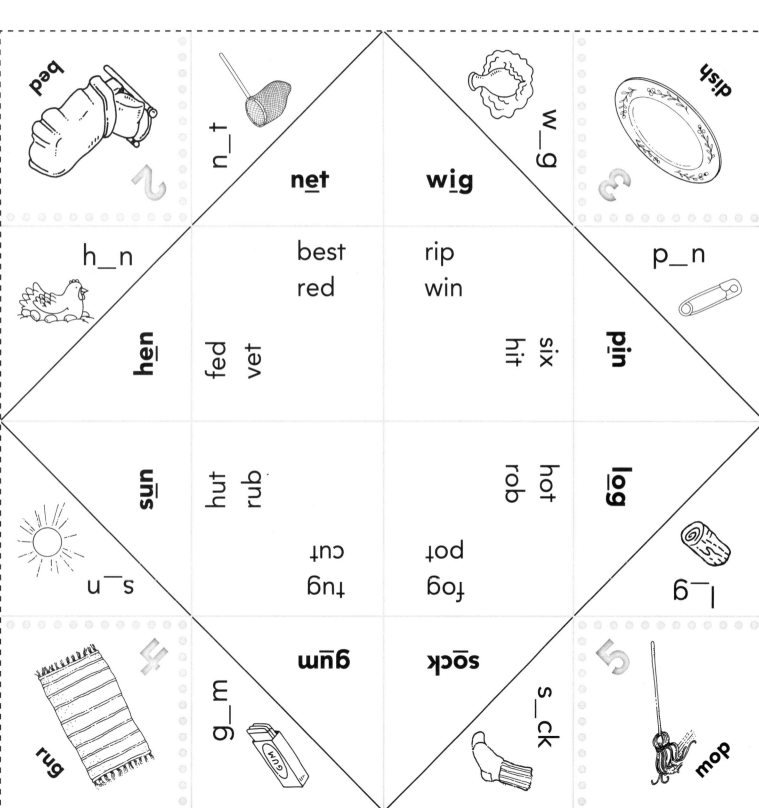

bed

2

n_t

net

wig

w_g

dish

3

h_n

best
red

rip
win

p_n

hen

fed
vet

six
hit

pin

sun

hut
rub

hot
rob

log

u_s

cut
tug

pot
fog

l_g

rug

4

g_m

gum

sock

s_ck

mop

5

13 Traveling Along

Name the picture. Add the vowel sound.
Pick your favorite way to travel to start.

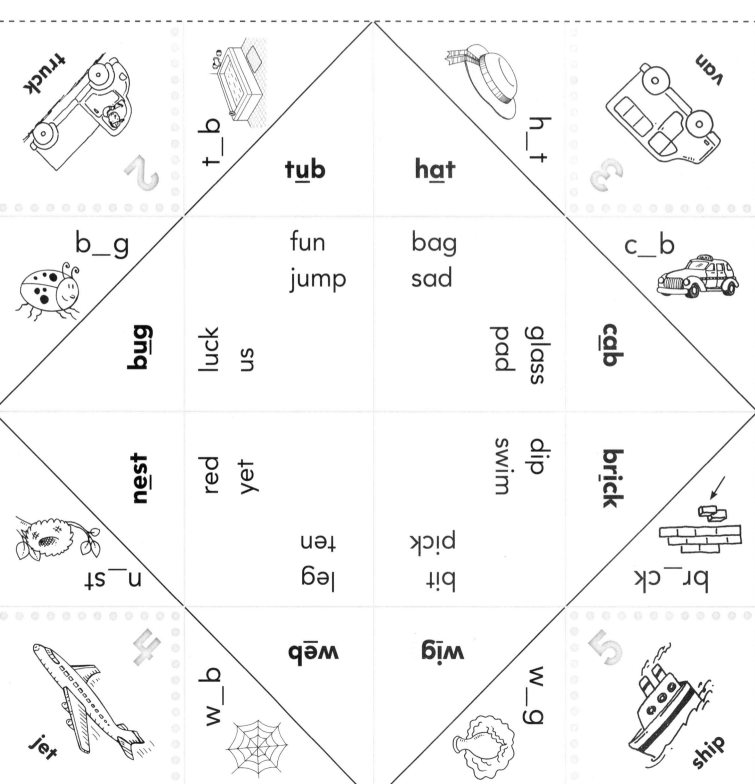

truck

2

t_b

tub

fun
jump

bug

luck
us

b_g

nest

red
yet

n_st

jet

4

w_b

web

ten
leg

wig

pick
bit

w_g

ship

5

br_ck

brick

swim
dip

cab

glass
pad

c_b

van

3

h_t

hat

bag
sad

14 Dressing Baby

Name the picture. Add the vowel sound.
Pick your favorite kind of baby clothes to start.

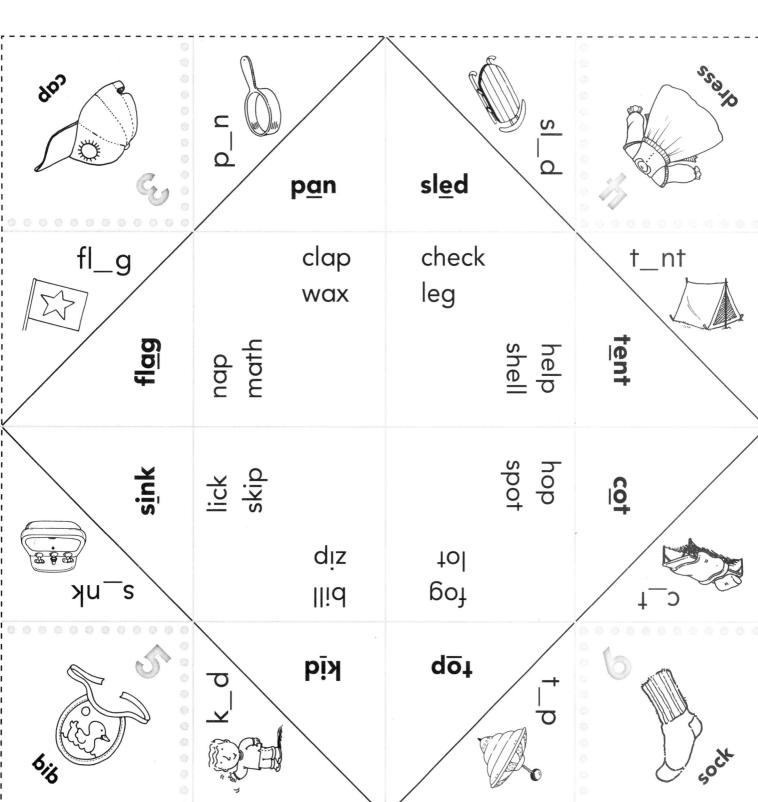

cap

3

p_n

sl_d

dress

4

fl_g

pan

sled

t_nt

clap
wax

check
leg

flag

nap   math

shell   help

tent

sink

lick   skip

hop   spot

cat

s_nk

zip
bill

lot
fog

c_t

bib

5

k_d

kid

top

t_p

6

sock

15 Animal Homes

Name the picture. Add the vowel sound.
Pick your favorite animal home to start.

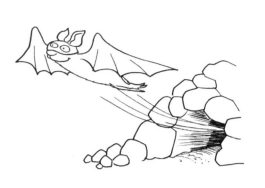

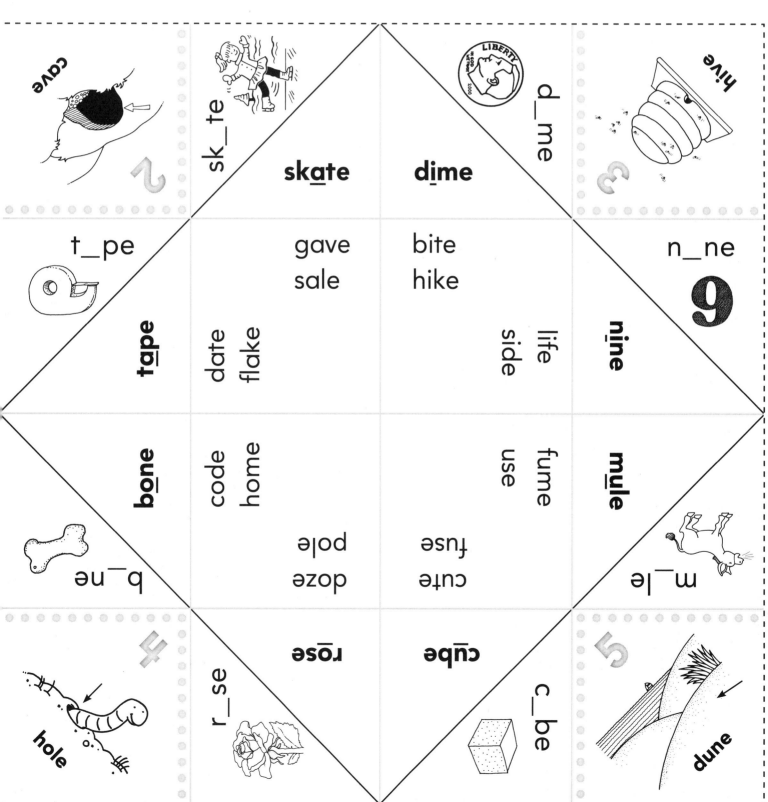

cave

sk_te

sk**a**te

d_me

d**i**me

hive

t_pe

gave
sale

bite
hike

n_ne

9

t**a**pe

date
flake

life
side

n**i**ne

b**o**ne

code
home

fume
use

m**u**le

b_ne

pole
doze

cute
fuse

m_le

hole

r_se

r**o**se

c**u**be

c_be

dune

16 All for Fun

Name the picture. Add the vowel sound.
Pick your favorite fun thing to start.

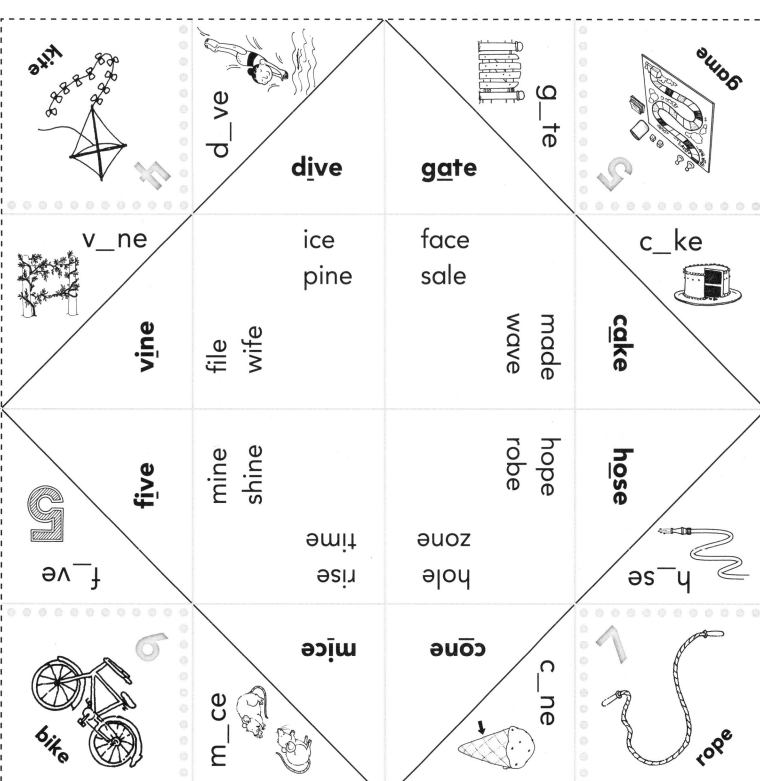

kite

d_ve

g_te

game

4

5

v_ne

dive

gate

c_ke

ice
pine

face
sale

vine

file   wife

made
wave

cake

five

mine   shine

hope
robe

hose

5

time
rise

zone
hole

f_ve

mice

cone

h_se

bike

m_ce

c_ne

rope

6

7

17 Helpful Holders

Name the picture. Add the vowel sound.
Pick your favorite container to start.

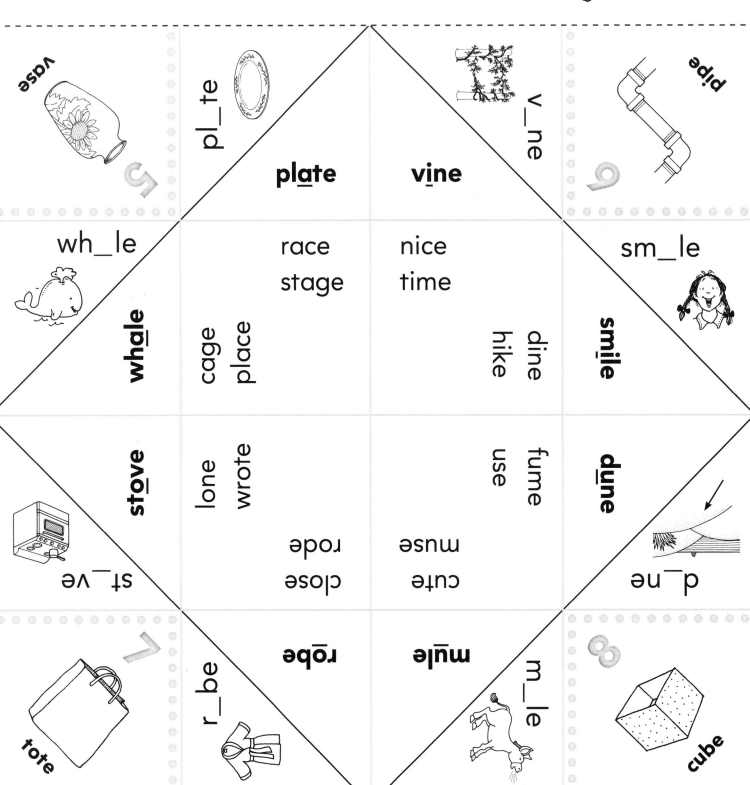

vase

pl_te

plate

vine

v_ne

pipe

wh_le

whale

race
stage

cage
place

nice
time

dine
hike

smile

sm_le

stove

lone
wrote

fume
use

dune

st_ve

rode
close

cute
muse

d_ne

tote

r_be

robe

mule

m_le

cube

18 All Wet

Name the picture. Add the vowel sound.
Pick your favorite wet thing to start.

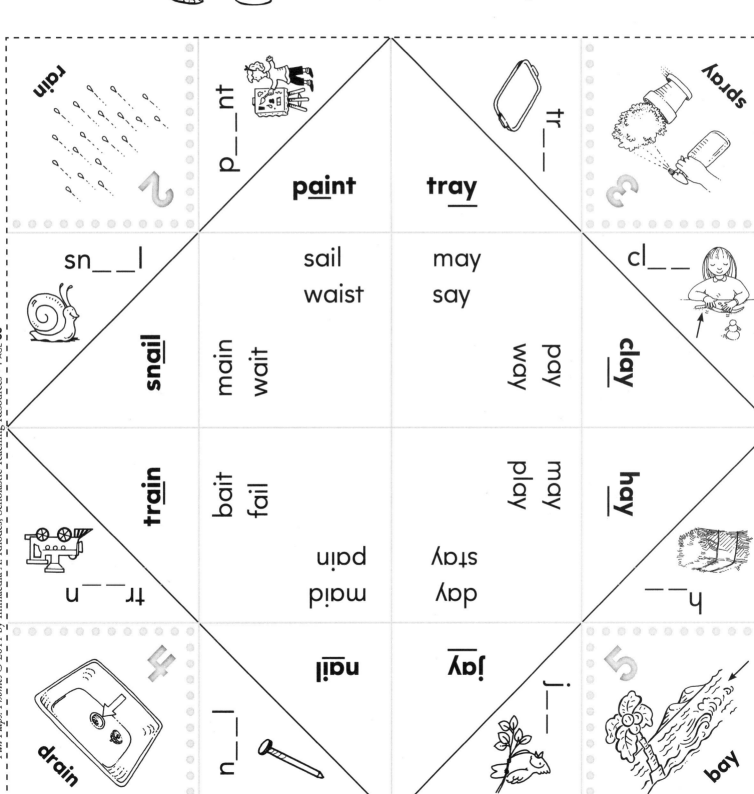

rain
2

p__nt

paint

tray

tr___

spray
3

sn___l

sail
waist

may
say

cl___

snail

main
wait

pay
way

clay

train

bait
fail

may
play

hay

tr___n

pain
maid

day
stay

h___

drain
4

n__l

nail

jay

j___

bay
5

19 Going for a Ride

Name the picture. Add the vowel sound.
Pick your favorite picture about going for a ride to start.

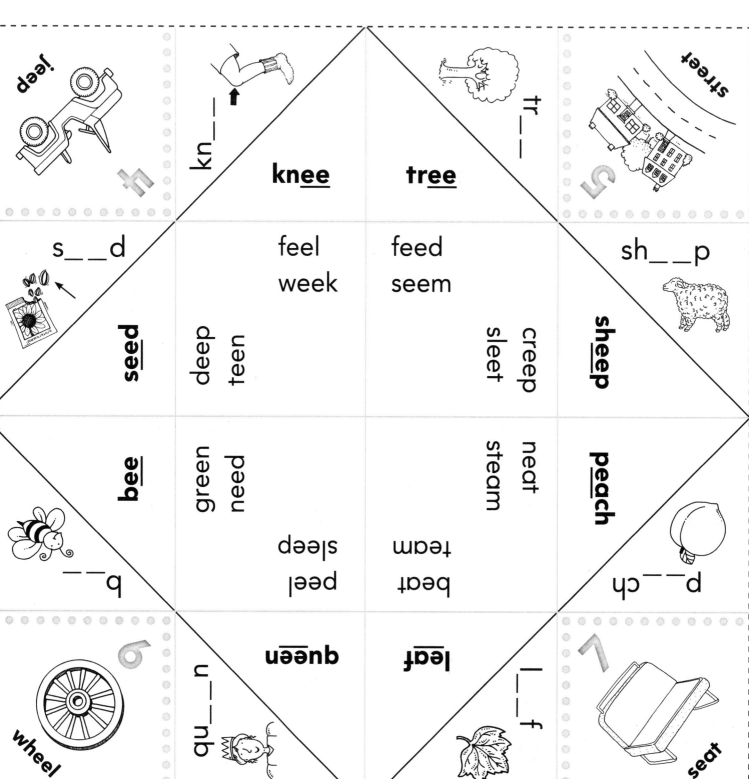

jeep

4

kn__

knee

tree

tr__

3

street

s __ __ d

feel
week

feed
seem

sh__p

seed

deep
teen

creep
sleet

sheep

bee

green
need

neat
steam

peach

b__

sleep
peel

beat
team

p__ch

wheel

6

qu__n

queen

leaf

l__f

7

seat

20 Wintry Day

Name the picture. Add the vowel sound.
Pick your favorite winter thing to start.

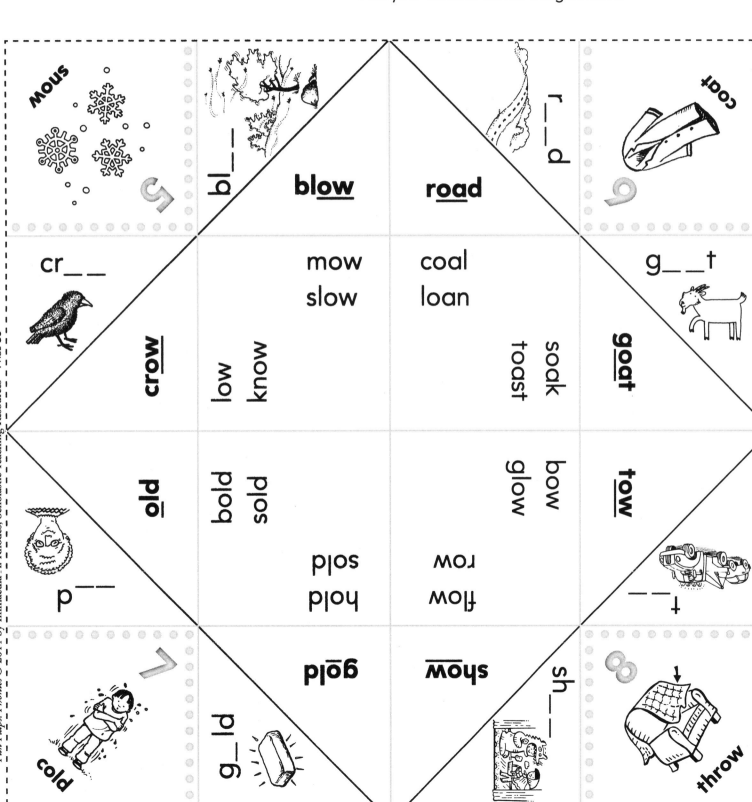

snow

sn_ _

5

bl_ _

blow

mow
slow

crow

cr_ _ _

low   know

old

bold   sold

p_ _ d

sold
hold

gold

g_ld

cold

7

road

road

coal
loan

soak
toast

bow
glow

row
flow

show

sh_ _

r_ _ d

coat

6

g_ _ t

goat

tow

t_ _ _

throw

8

21 Working the Farm

Name the picture. Add the vowel sound.
Pick your favorite picture to start.

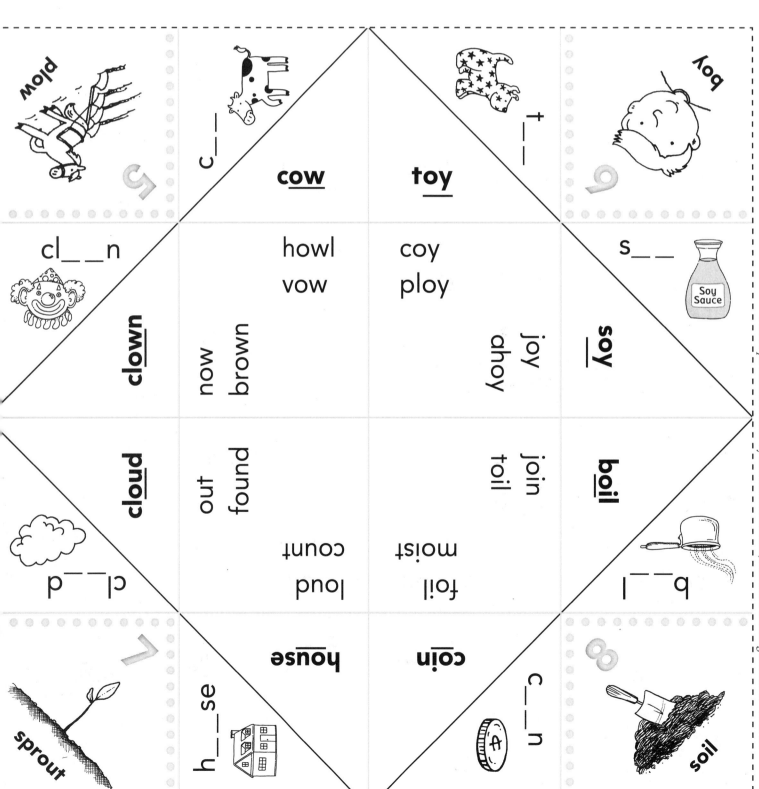

plow
5

c_ _

cow

toy

t_ _

boy
6

cl_ _n

howl
vow

coy
ploy

s_ _ _

Soy
Sauce

clown

now   brown

joy   ahoy

soy

cloud

out   found

join   toil

boil

p_ _d

count   loud

moist   foil

b_ _l

sprout
7

h_ _se

house

coin

c_ _n

soil
8

22 Places to Go

Name the picture. Add the vowel sound.
Pick the place you would most like to visit to start.

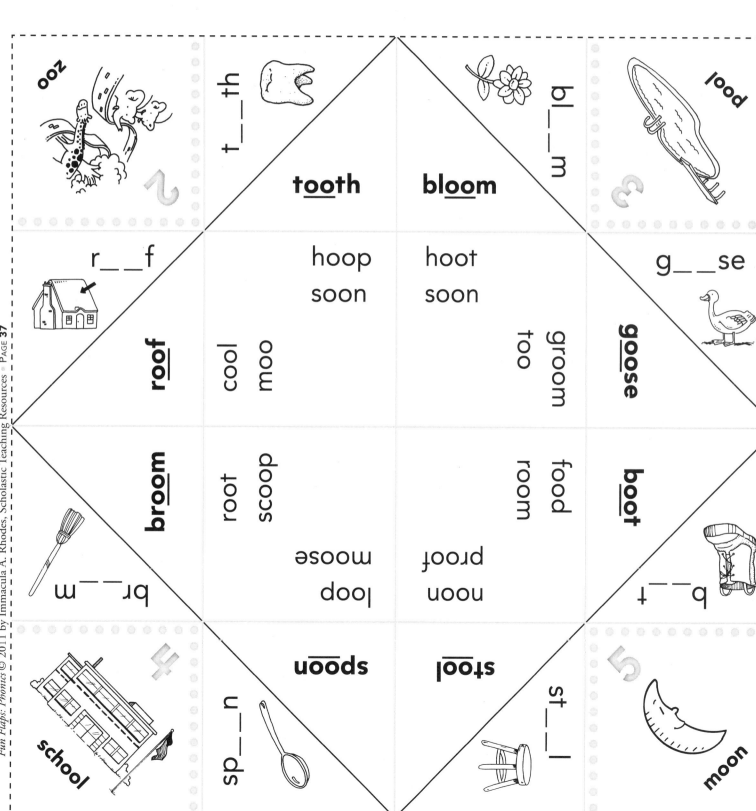

z_oo

t__th

tooth

bloom

bl__m

pool

r__f

hoop
soon

hoot
soon

g___se

roof

cool
moo

groom
too

goose

broom

root
scoop

food
room

boot

br__m

moose
loop

proof
noon

b__t

school

sp__n

spoon

stool

st__l

moon

23 In Fashion

Name the picture. Add the vowel sound.
Pick your favorite fashion item to start.

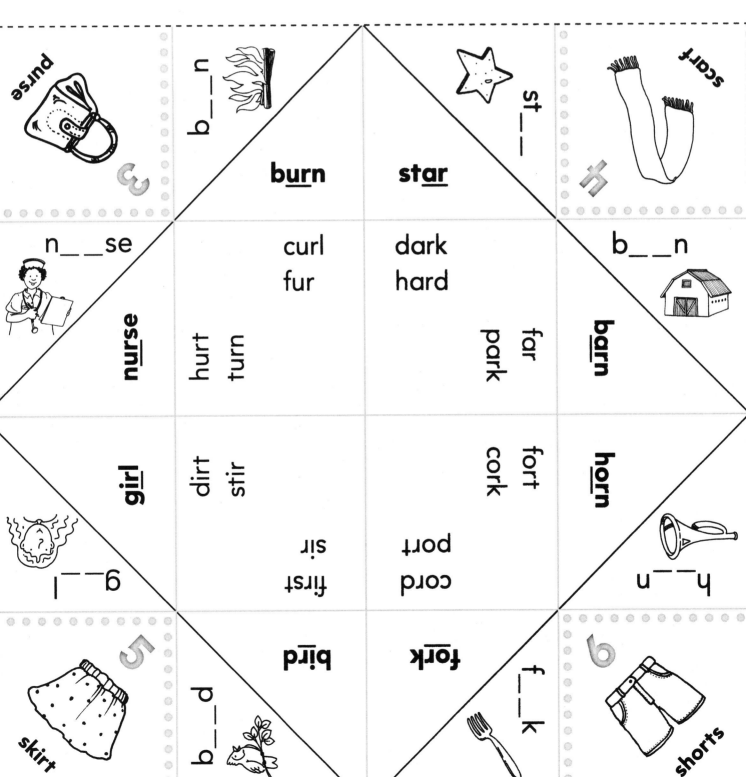

purse

3

b_ _n

burn

star

st_ _

scarf

4

n_ _se

curl
fur

dark
hard

b_ _ _n

nurse

hurt
turn

far
park

barn

girl

dirt
stir

fort
cork

horn

g_ _l

sir
first

port
cord

h_ _n

5
skirt

b_ _d
bird

fork

f_ _k

6
shorts

24 City Sights

Name the picture. Add the vowel sound.
Pick your favorite city sight to start.

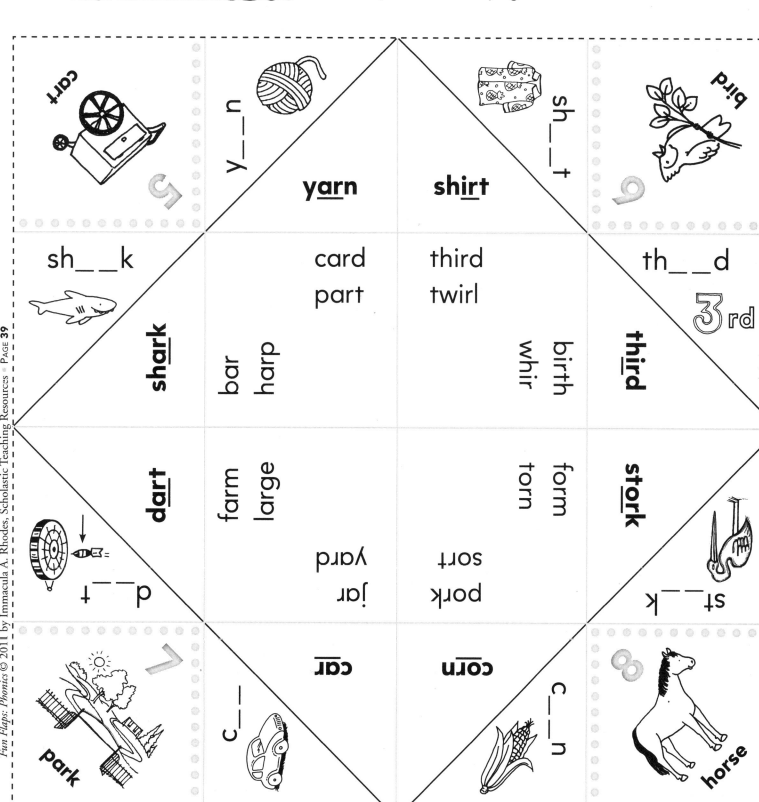

cart

y__n

yarn

shirt

sh__t

bird

5

6

sh__ _k

card
part

third
twirl

th_ _ _d

3rd

shark

bar
harp

birth
whir

third

dart

farm
large

form
torn

stork

d_ _t

yard
jar

pork
sort

st_ _k

park

7

car

c_ _

corn

c_ _n

8

horse

25 The Great Outdoors

Name the picture. Add the beginning sound.
Pick your favorite outdoor thing to start.

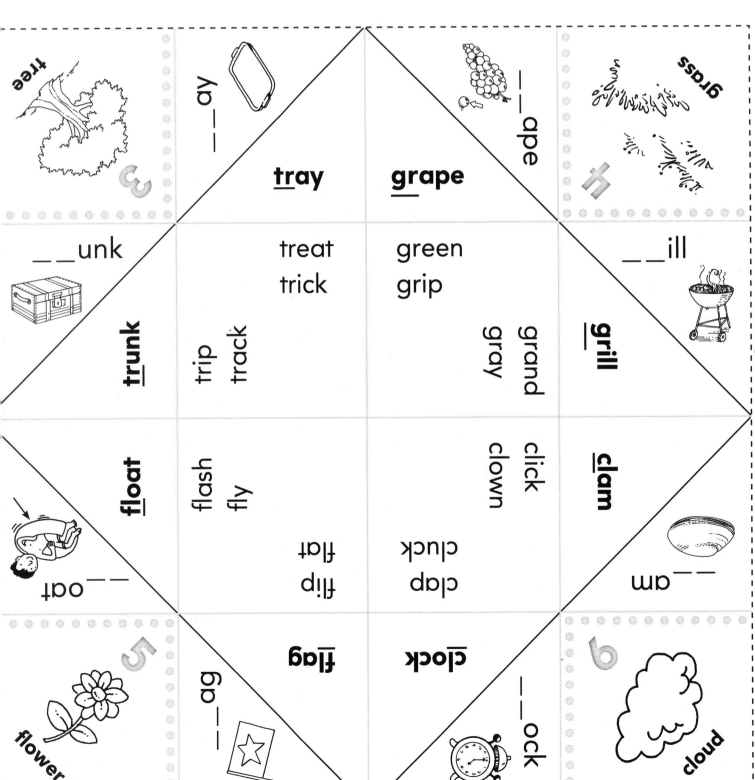

tree

3

__ay

tray   grape

__ape

grass

4

__unk

treat
trick

green
grip

__ill

trunk

trip   track

grand
gray

grill

float

flash
fly

click
clown

clam

__oat

flip   flat

clap   cluck

__am

5

flower

__ag

flag   clock

__ock

6

cloud

26 Making Music

Name the picture. Add the beginning sound.
Pick your favorite instrument to start.

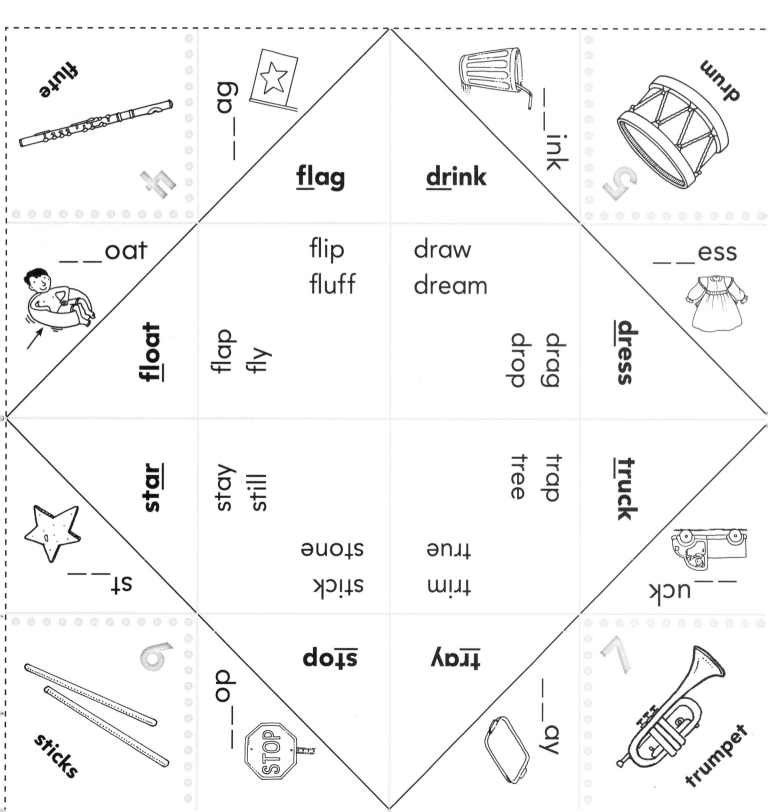

flute

___ag

flag   **drink**

___ink

drum

5

___oat

flip
fluff

draw
dream

___ess

float

flap
fly

drag
drop

dress

star

stay
still

tree
trap

truck

st___

stick
stone

trim
true

___uck

6

___op

stop   **tray**

___ay

7

sticks

trumpet

27 Let's Play!

Name the picture. Add the beginning sound.
Pick your favorite way to play to start.

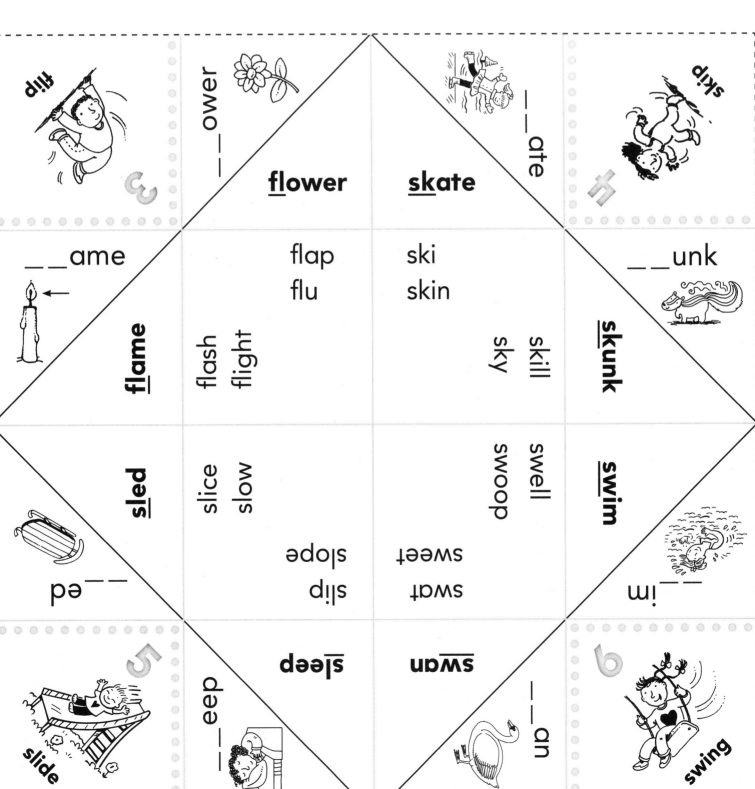

3 flip

__ower

flower

skate

__ate

4 skip

__ame

flame

flap
flu

ski
skin

__unk

flash
flight

sled

slice
slow

skill
sky

skunk

swell
swoop

swim

__ed

slip
slope

swat
sweet

__im

5 slide

__eep

sleep

swan

__an

6 swing

28 In the Kingdom

Name the picture. Add the beginning sound.
Pick your favorite kingdom-related thing to start.

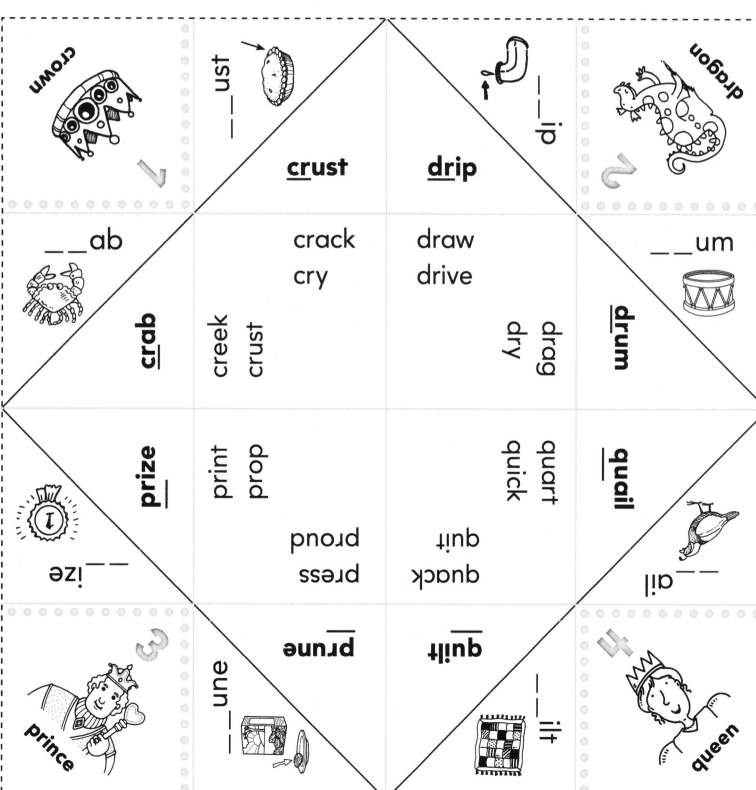

29 Cool Critters

Name the picture. Add the beginning sound.
Pick your favorite critter to start.

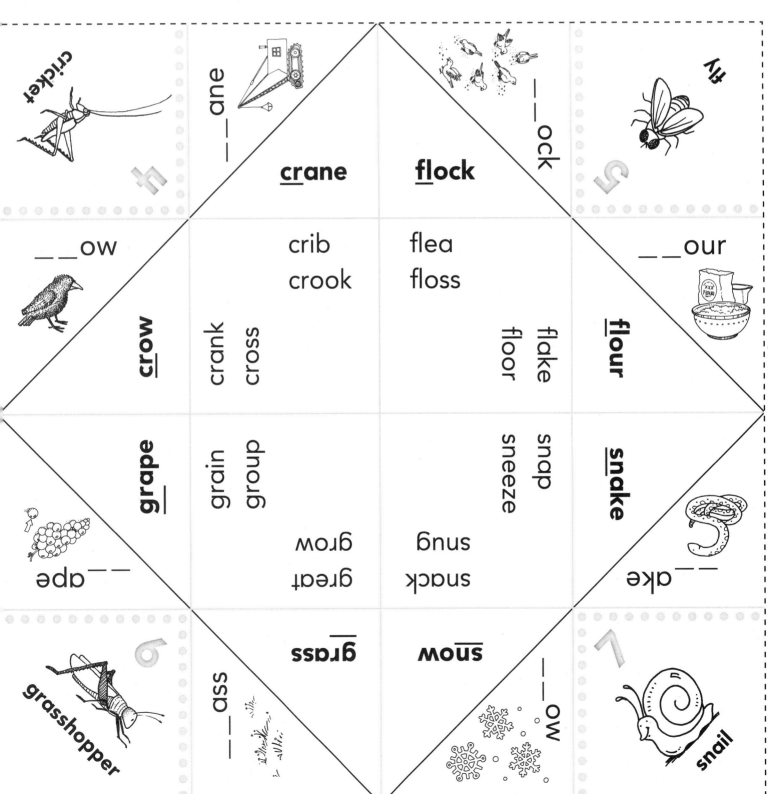

cricket

__ane

__ock

fly

4

5

crane

flock

__ow

__our

crow

crib
crook

flea
floss

crank cross

flake
floor

flour

grape

grain group

snap
sneeze

snake

ape

great
grow

snack
snug

ake

grasshopper

grass

snow

snail

6

ass

ow

7

30 Ready to Eat

Name the picture. Add the beginning sound.
Pick your favorite eating item to start.

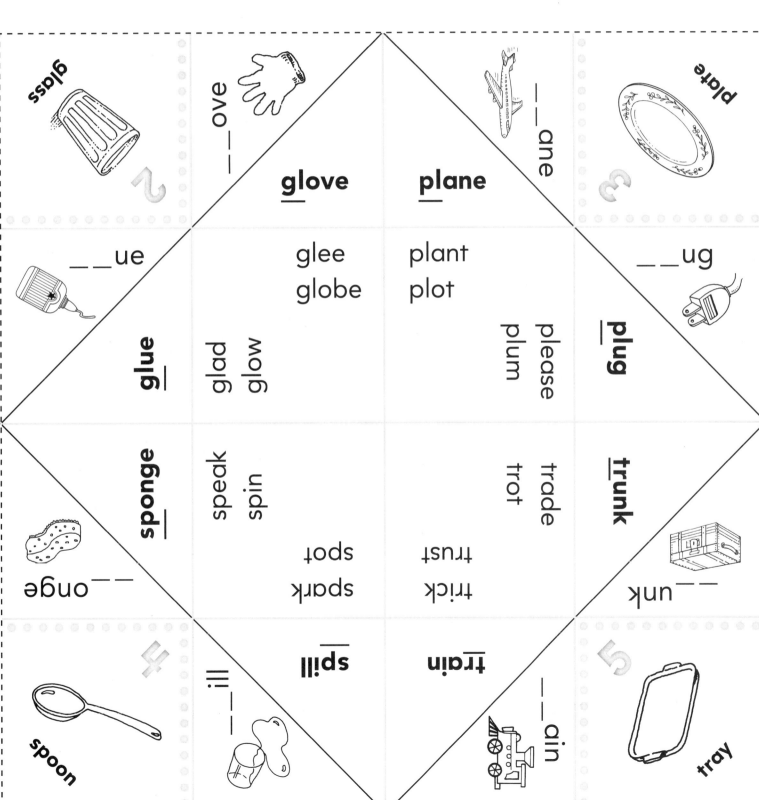

glass

2

__ove

glove

plane

__ane

plate

3

__ue

glee
globe

plant
plot

__ug

glue

glad
glow

please
plum

plug

sponge

speak
spin

trade
trot

trunk

__onge

spot
spark

trust
trick

__unk

4

__ill

spill

train

__ain

5

spoon

tray

31 Little Things

Name the picture. Add the beginning sound.
Pick your favorite little thing to start.

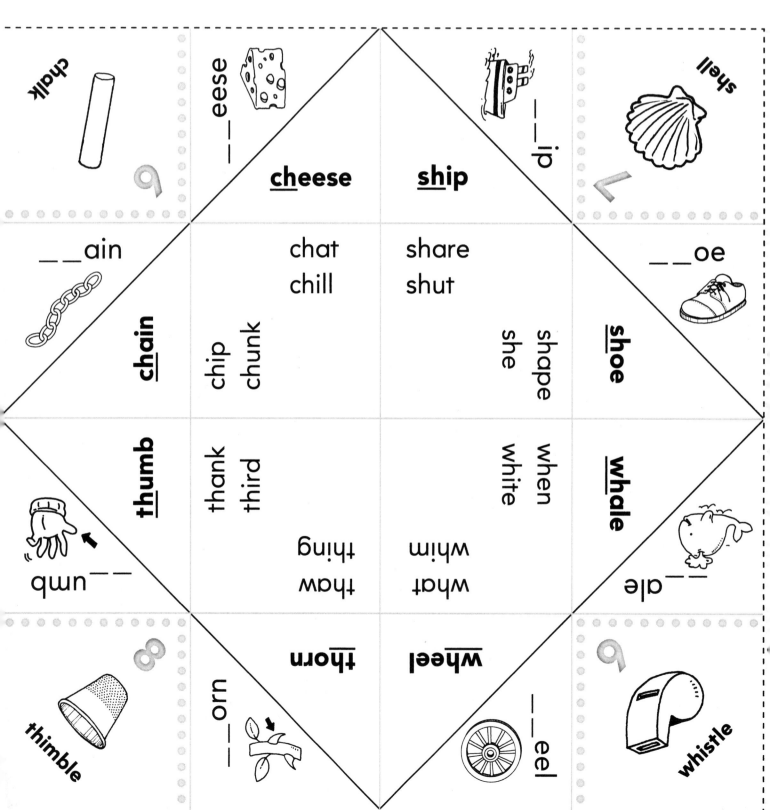

chalk

__eese

__ip

shell

__ain

chain

chat
chill

chip chunk

cheese

ship

share
shut

shape
she

shoe

__oe

thumb

thank
third

thing
thaw

when
white

whim
what

whale

qun__ __

thorn

wheel

__ale

__orn

thimble

__eel

whistle

32 All About Tools

Name the picture. Add the beginning sound.
Pick your favorite tool-related item to start.

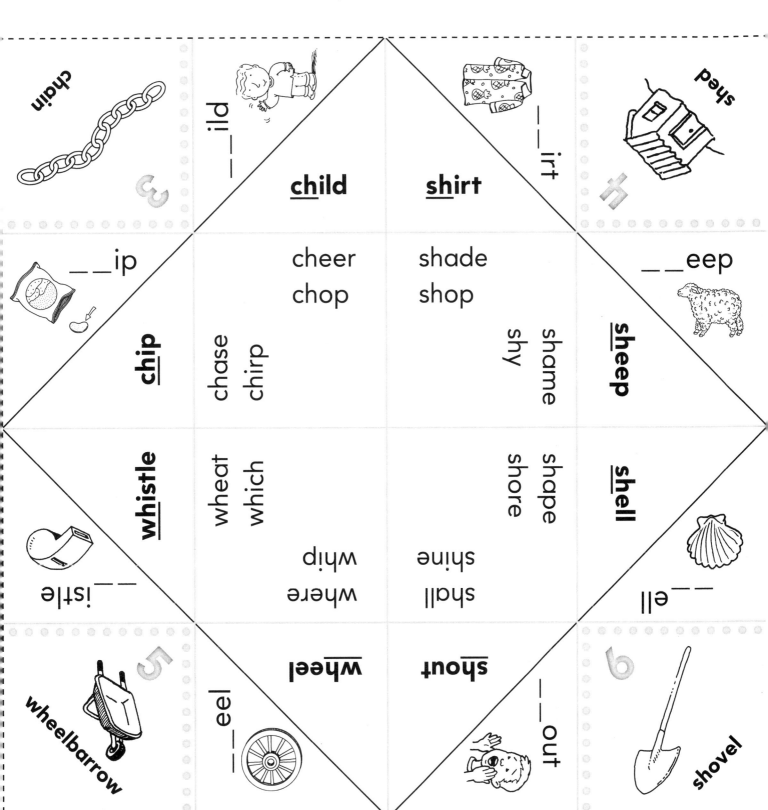

chain

3

__ild

child   **shirt**

__irt

shed

4

__ip

cheer   shade
chop   shop

__eep

chip   chase   shame   **sheep**
              chirp   shy

whistle   wheat   shape   **shell**
               which   shore

__istle   where   shall
               whip   shine

wheel   **shout**

5

__eel

__out

wheelbarrow

6

__ell

shovel

Fun Flap Template

Make your own fun flap!

❶ Choose a phonics skill. Draw (or glue) a picture for a different skill in each corner. Write a number from 2 to 9 in each circle.

❷ Draw two more pictures for each phonics skill in the spaces next to your first picture. Use the fun flaps in this book as a guide.

❸ Write words that represent each phonics skill on the set of lines near the center of your fun flap.

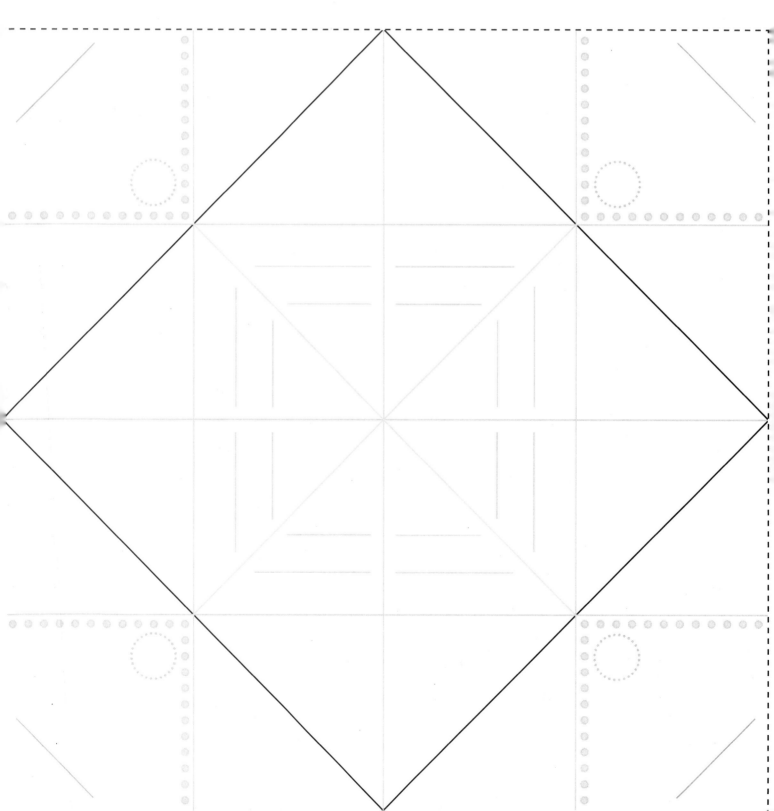